ZERO PLEASURES

ZERO PLEASURES

Ayana Thakran

Bigfoot Publications

Because, there's a writer in everyone.

Zero Pleasures

Author : Ayana Thakran

First Published by

Bigfoot06 Publications (OPC) Pvt. Ltd.

1st floor, BSR Building near Vishal Mega Mart,

Daultabad Flyover, Laxman Vihar Phase 3,

Gurugram, Haryana (122001)

Website: www.bigfootpublications.in

Email: info@bigfootpublications.in

First Edition : December, 2023

ISBN Print Book - **978-81-19512-50-8**

Typeset in Bell MT 12pt

by Yachika Prajapati For Bigfoot06 Publication

Printed in India

There is more joy and fulfilment in pursuing less than can be found in pursuing more – Joshua Fields Millburn

Dedication

I dedicate this book to my teenage friends who may have a strong urge to constantly check on their phones, and get drawn towards the path of achieving momentary highs in their lives, even by being validated by social media, and by basking in false sense of pride.

I also dedicate it to my mother **Dr. Priyanka Thakran***, who has always believed in me and inspired me to be my true self, my maternal grandmother* **Mrs. Kamlesh Thakran***, who remained my biggest critic, my maternal grandfather* **Mr. Suresh Thakran***, who is an eminent Hindi writer, and my sweet younger brother* **Mast. Viraj Thakran***, who practically left no stone unturned in trying to distract me. Special thanks to my friend cum mentor, my uncle,* **Mr. Manish Chaudhary***.*

This book revolves around the journey embarked by a fictional character of a teenage girl Elsa Reed, also beautifully depicting subjective analysis of an objective issue. The author does not intend to hurt anyone's emotions or to preach any particular ideology.

FOREWORD

"Desires make slaves out of kings and patience makes kings out of slaves." This insightful quote succinctly encapsulates the core theme of the book at hand, wherein the author embarks on a profound exploration of the intricate interplay between human desires and the virtuous quality of patience. With masterful storytelling, the author skillfully dissects the dichotomy of ambition and self-control, weaving a compelling narrative that invites readers to question conventional wisdom.

Furthermore, this book does not merely dwell in the realm of theory; it offers pragmatic insights and actionable strategies for individuals to harness the transformative power of patience in their own lives. In a world often driven by instant gratification, the wisdom imparted within these pages serves as a beacon of enlightenment and self-improvement. Readers will undoubtedly find themselves both captivated and enriched by the profound wisdom and practical guidance found within these chapters.

Dr. Savita Arora

Principal (National Awardee)

Bharti Public School

Table of Contents

Exordium

"Desires make slaves out of kings and patience makes kings out of slaves", Al- Ghazali, a famous stoic philosopher quoted.

Pleasure is the transient state or feeling of being pleased, gratified or delighted by anything or any act. On the other hand, "a state of zero pleasures!" does not mean being detached from all the pleasures of the world in its literal sense. Instead, it means achieving a state of equanimity and trust in the longevity of the process that leads to lasting sense of fulfilment and contentment.

Difference between 'Nihil' and 'Zero'

Nihilism, derived from the Latin word "nihil" meaning "nothing," is a philosophical perspective that denies the existence of any objective or inherent meaning in life. According to nihilism, all moral, social, and religious values are baseless and devoid of intrinsic significance. On the contrary, the idea of zero pleasures arises from the belief that any pleasures we experience in life are ultimately transient and inconsequential in the grand scheme of things.

Embracing the notion of no pleasures can have profound implications for human existence. If life lacks inherent meaning, then our pursuits of pleasure, success, and happiness become mere distractions from the underlying truth. Nihilism can lead to feelings of existential despair, apathy, and a sense of futility in striving for pleasure or fulfilment. However, a state of zero pleasure, according to the author, is a state of 'emotional balance' and 'core satisfaction'.

"Too oft is transient pleasure the source of long woes": German Poet Christoph Martin Wieland.

Therefore, some may interpret the idea of zero pleasures as liberating, freeing individuals from the burden of constantly seeking happiness and pleasure. Instead of focusing on transient and instant gratifications, one might turn their attention to understanding the world, exploring personal interests, or connecting with others on a deeper level. In response to the absence of inherent meaning, individuals have the opportunity to create their own subjective meanings and values by:

1. Embracing Absurdity: The philosopher Albert Camus argued that humans must confront the inherent absurdity of life and embrace it. By acknowledging the lack of ultimate purpose, individuals can find value in their actions and choices, regardless of whether they lead to pleasure or not.

2. Pursuit of Authenticity: Instead of seeking pleasures that may be fleeting and unfulfilling, individuals can focus on living authentically and aligning their actions with their true values and beliefs.

3. Contribution to Others: Finding meaning can also come from contributing to the well-being of others and society. Acts of kindness, compassion, and empathy can provide a sense of purpose that transcends individual pleasures.

4. Personal Growth and Fulfilment: Engaging in constant self-improvement, intellectual pursuits, and creative endeavours can offer a sense of fulfilment that goes beyond momentary pleasures.

For *Elsa Reed,* it has been a thought-provoking and heartfelt journey of self- discovery and growth. Elsa's unique transformation as a teenage girl challenges conventional ideas of happiness, encouraging readers to find meaning and fulfilment beyond the pursuit of fleeting pleasures. A book that resonates with both teenagers and adults alike, *Zero Pleasures* strongly reminds us of the power that lies in embracing our authenticity and living a purposeful life.

Elsa Lived the Life of a Princess

"Up and about! It's time for school!" honked the digital alarm clock that sat hesitant on the bedside table of Elsa. It was Friday morning and Elsa was not in a mood to go to school today. "Fridays are too boring", hushed Elsa, as she threw her velvet sheet off her lazy body.

"Make something interesting for breakfast!", she shouted out to her house helps, "I am fed up of eating the same thing every Friday", she yelled out to them again as she rushed to her splendid shower room.

Elsa Reed was a teenage girl who according to her friends and teachers, was born with a silver spoon in her mouth. She was raised in an effluent family. Her father, Mr. Marcus Reed used to be a famous soccer player and her mother Mrs. Neha Sharma Reed, originally an Indian, owns a chain of spa centres called "Luxe Spa", in and outside the town where many eminent Hollywood celebrities visit to strike a balance in their hefty earnings. The family now lives in the posh Beverly Hills in California.

Elsa's world seemed to revolve around the constant pursuit of pleasure. From the beginning of her life, Elsa had seen a modern household with almost all the facilities and a luxurious lifestyle. Being the only child of her parents, Elsa was pampered tremendously. She had various servants in her house who were always on their toes to provide Elsa the best of livelihood. An exotic collection laid in her wardrobe with magnificent charm of beautiful ballerinas. Elsa was quite influenced by all the pomp and show the celebrities visiting her mother's spa centres carried with their aura.

As the first rays of sunlight peeked through her window, Elsa would rise with an eager anticipation for the pleasures that awaited her. The moment she woke up each day, her thoughts were consumed with seeking enjoyment and avoiding anything that might bring even the slightest discomfort. Her life had become a carousel of indulgence, constantly spinning in search of momentary highs. Decadent treats adorned her breakfast table, each bite a fleeting taste of ecstasy that momentarily numbed the mundanity of everyday life. The flavours danced upon her taste buds, offering a brief escape from the humdrum routine.

Throughout the day, she was a captive of her desires, unable to resist the allure of her favourite shows that beckoned from the screen. With each episode, she was whisked away into fictional worlds of drama and fantasy, losing herself in a world far removed from her own.

But perhaps her most loyal companion was her smartphone, a tiny device that held an entire universe of entertainment at her fingertips. Elsa's days were spent incessantly scrolling through her social media feed, seeking the thrill of validation through the likes, comments, and emojis that adorned her posts.

Each heart or thumbs-up was like a burst of euphoria, momentarily satisfying her hunger for approval and recognition. It was as if the number of virtual hearts she received validated her worth in the digital realm, even though she couldn't help but wonder if these moments of affirmation were fleeting and superficial.

Yet, despite the constant pursuit of pleasure, as a growing teen, Elsa couldn't escape an unshakable feeling of emptiness deep within her soul. The fleeting moments of joy never seemed to quench her thirst for lasting contentment. It was like trying to fill an endless chasm with fleeting drops of water, leaving her feeling parched for something more substantial.

In the midst of her hedonistic lifestyle, Elsa couldn't ignore the growing void inside her. She wondered if this relentless chase for pleasure was merely a distraction—a way to avoid confronting her own vulnerabilities and insecurities. Perhaps these fleeting moments of delight were a mask to shield herself from the discomfort of self-reflection and personal growth.

From the allure of social media to the enticing world of material possessions, Elsa had fallen into the trap of believing that happiness was synonymous with pleasure. The more she indulged in these momentary joys, the more she craved them, convinced that they held the key to lasting fulfilment. Poor fellow! She remained entrapped into this vicious cycle of achieving and desiring or longing for more.

Gradually, Elsa began to sense an underlying emptiness. It was as if the pursuit of pleasure was a never-ending quest, leaving her yearning for more, yet never fully satisfied. She couldn't shake off the feeling that something was missing from her life—a void that pleasure alone could not fill.

Her desires for the pleasures had gone to the extent that she did not even wish to appear for her exams, fearing that her result would probably open her eyes one day to a world full of utter discomfort. Due to this she even pretended to be unwell during the exams of some particular subjects that she used to struggle with.

As the weeks turned into months, Elsa found herself at a crossroads, contemplating the true source of her happiness. A new feeling enveloped her that her life couldn't revolve solely around the pursuit of pleasure. Something deeper and more meaningful called to her—a call to discover a sense of fulfilment that extended beyond the transient highs of indulgence.

This phase in Elsa's life marked a turning point—a realization that the pursuit of pleasure alone couldn't fill the void within her. It was time for her to embark on a journey of self-discovery, seeking to understand the root of her relentless pursuit and finding a deeper and more authentic sense of happiness—one that transcended the fleeting allure of instant gratification. Though Elsa was not oblivious of this, but she wished to remain ignorant with this fact as the momentary tickle of her pleasures gave her soul episodic outbursts of laughter.

In the bustling world of adolescence, Elsa found herself entangled in this pursuit of pleasure. Like a whirlwind, her days were filled with seeking out moments of instant gratification, chasing after fleeting highs that seemed to fade as quickly as they came. She wanted to remain far away from embracing the challenges, confronting her emotions, and finding joy in the little moments that life had to offer. Hardly did she know, that it was a journey of growth, resilience, and courage—a journey towards a life beyond the mere pursuit of pleasure, that was awaiting her.

Cognitive Shift

One evening, as Elsa sat in her room scrolling through social media, she stumbled upon a quote that resonated with her deeply: *"Happiness is not a destination; it is a way of life."* Intrigued by the words, she felt an urge to understand their true meaning. With curiosity ignited, Elsa embarked on a journey of introspection. She began to question her motives and pondered the consequences of a life solely defined by pleasure-seeking. Was she using these fleeting moments of joy as an escape from facing her own insecurities and fears? Was her pursuit of pleasure a way to mask her true feelings of vulnerability and uncertainty? The questions shook her mind.

Through moments of quiet reflection, Elsa recognized that her relentless pursuit of pleasure was indeed a way of avoiding her deeper emotions. She had been using these distractions as a shield to protect herself from the discomfort that often accompanies self-exploration and growth. Determined to break free from this cycle, Elsa made a conscious decision to redefine her approach to happiness. Instead of seeking momentary happiness, she started to explore what brought her a sense of true fulfilment and lasting joy.

During this Christmas vacations, Elsa started spending more time with her parents. She got mingled with her house helps and learnt a few things to cook this Christmas. She enjoyed wonderful decorations and the colourful lights in the streets outside. There was some kind of happiness in the air as the Christmas was near.

The happy faces on the streets gave her goosebumps as she realised that it has been long since she felt so connected to her surroundings.

She discovered that spending quality time with loved ones, engaging in her hobbies, and pursuing her passions ignited a different kind of happiness within her—an authentic and soulful joy that extended beyond the temporary pleasures she had been accustomed to.

As Elsa began to shift her focus from the pursuit of pleasure to a life of purpose and meaning, she found herself savouring the beauty of simple moments. A warm cup of tea on a rainy day, a heartwarming conversation with a friend, or a breathtaking sunset became sources of genuine happiness for her.

The journey was not without its challenges. Elsa faced moments of temptation, especially when her peers indulged in their favourite pleasures. But she was determined to stay true to her newfound path of purposeful living. With time, Elsa felt a newfound sense of contentment and peace within herself. She learned that true happiness came from living a life guided by her values, embracing her vulnerabilities, and finding joy in the journey of self-discovery.

She broke free from the confines of a life defined by pleasure and embraced a path of authentic happiness—*a life of Zero Pleasures*. She realized that happiness was not an external destination to be reached but a way of living, anchored in meaningful connections, personal growth, and embracing life's challenges with resilience and courage.

As Elsa continued her journey of self-discovery, she found herself less bound by the fleeting allure of pleasure and she started realising the radiance in the light of a life filled with purpose, meaning, and fulfilment. She started to realise that many of us are just trapped souls in the cages of our minds.

An Unexpected Encounter

One fateful day, as Elsa idly scrolled through her phone during a particularly dull class, her eyes got stuck to an ironical quote that fortunately set her on a path of introspection and self-discovery. The words appeared on her screen, anonymous and cryptic, yet they held a mysterious allure: *"Find your pleasures in facing your fears."*

Intrigued by the quote, Elsa's curiosity was piqued. Who could have written this enigmatic missive, and what did it truly mean? Despite her attempts to trace the writer, the digital trail led to a dead-end, leaving her with only the lingering questions that the message had sparked.

Unable to shake off the feeling that this message held a deeper significance, Elsa decided to embrace the idea of exploring its meaning. She felt an instant stirring within her, a yearning to uncover the secret behind those few words. Could there be more to life than the fleeting pleasures she had been chasing? And could such a self-discovery hold the key to true fulfilment? Could in any way our fears lead to pleasures? Elsa was drawn towards thinking about her extreme fear of failing in her subjects! Could facing this fear of mine lead to pleasures as well? The question ignited a new thought process altogether.

With a newfound sense of purpose, Elsa began her quest for understanding. She delved into books, articles, and online forums, searching for wisdom that resonated with the cryptic message. It was during one of her explorations that she stumbled upon an old, hidden gem—a quaint bookstore tucked away in the corner of the city.

As she stepped inside the cozy establishment, a sense of intrigue enveloped her. The bookstore seemed to hold secrets of ages past, waiting to be unravelled by those with an open mind and a curious heart. And it was there, amid the scent of aging paper and the soft murmur of turning pages, that Esa encountered something beautiful and attractive. Feeling a little misplaced at the shop, Elsa looked around and found a charismatic brown-eyed tall girl with long dark brown hair who was trying hard to wave and call Elsa from outside the glass door of the book shop. As Elsa walked outside, she observed that though the girl looked a bit hesitant, she was pretty confident. She exuded an air of wisdom and serenity, her eyes reflecting the depths of her life experiences. They shared an instant connection, as if the universe had conspired to bring them together at this precise moment. Her mother used to say, "your energy introduces you even before you speak!", thought Elsa, stunned by the enigma of the girl outside.

"Hey! My name is Mia" said the girl who tried to introduce herself before asking Elsa for a favour. "Hi!" said Elsa, "What can I do for you?" she asked, trying to help. "I am a tourist here. I am from India. I am fond of interesting and inspirational books and the shop caught my attention. But the board outside says clothes above knee aren't allowed inside the premises. Could you just help me if there are a few good inspirational books on Buddhism inside. I shall pay from here and would love to buy a few if you could help." Mia continued. Elsa couldn't help her eyes off her face. She looked so attractive. There was definitely something charming about Mia that pulled Elsa's soul magnetically. "Oh! I would love to help!" said Elsa as she rushed inside to find a few books on the subject. Though Elsa could not understand such books and found them boring, but she tried to collect a few and brought them to Mia.

"Wonderful!" exclaimed Mia in ecstasy as she went through the books. Elsa felt a sense of pride within herself for having helped her and choosing the right books. As they conversed, Mia spoke in a manner that captivated Elsa's attention. "I shall buy both!" she said in a hurry. But Elsa wanted to talk to her. She asked where she was staying in Beverly Hills and said she would love to connect with her further. They exchanged their phone numbers and bid adieu.

As Elsa bid farewell to Mia and stepped back into the outside world, she thought she carried with her a newfound friend in Mia. On her ride back home, Elsa sent a few messages to Mia and expressed that she would like to meet her someday, if possible, at her home. Elsa was happy inviting Mia. Mia happily accepted the invitation and promised to see her an evening day after.

Elsa Invited Mia

Elsa was cheerful since she met Mia and was eagerly looking forward to see her at her home. She instructed her house helps to be courteous and decorate her bedroom and their drawing space well. She ordered her senior chef to prepare some exotic Indian dishes for Mia. She was so excited that she couldn't wait for the evening. It was a pleasure for her mother too.

When the clock finally struck 7:00, it was time for Mia to come. The door bell rang and Elsa ran to the door impatiently to welcome her new friend from India. Right at the entrance of her house stood Mia, with her vibrant smile, who carried a bouquet of lilies in her hand. Elsa grabbed the bouquet and saw that Mia had also brought a wrapped gift for her, that she insisted her to open once she leaves. Elsa readily agreed but curiosity started building up in her heart and mind. "After all, what could Mia have brought for me?" thought resonated in her mind.

Elsa welcomed Mia inside and both of them sat in the drawing space. "Your house looks resplendent!" said Mia, "it has a royal Indian charm", she couldn't stop herself from describing. Elsa introduced her mother to Mia and told her that she is originally an Indian. Mia respectfully touched her feet and Elsa's mom gave her blessings.

After a while, Elsa's mother called them for dinner and both of them sat at the dining table. Mia was positively surprised looking at the Indian cuisine and relished that. Elsa enjoyed the delicious food too, though it was a bit spicy for her.

During dinner, Mia shared her experience of reading inspirational books, her profound insights about life, happiness, and the pursuit of life's meaning. On the other hand, Elsa described her routine to Mia and discussed that though she lived a luxurious lifestyle and had an amazing family, but she felt a feeling of emptiness deep within her. Mia urged Elsa to look beyond the superficial pleasures of life and to seek joy in the exploration of her own inner world.

"True pleasure," Mia whispered with a gentle smile, "lies not in the fleeting highs of indulgence, but in the journey of self-discovery. It lies not in avoiding your fears, but in facing them with all the courage that you have! Embrace all that you are—the light and the shadows, the dreams and the fears. It is in knowing oneself that one can truly find contentment and purpose."

Those words resonated deeply within Elsa's soul. She felt as though a veil had been lifted, revealing a new perspective on life that she had never considered before. Mia encouraged her to embrace the highs and lows of her own being, to confront her fears and insecurities with courage, and to explore her passions beyond the allure of instant gratification.

She grabbed a sense of purpose and understanding. She realized that the pursuit of pleasure alone could never bring lasting fulfilment and pride. True joy lay in the journey of self-discovery, in understanding and embracing her authentic self, and in pursuing passions that brought her genuine fulfilment.

It was time for some sweet delicacies and Elsa did not realise when the clock struck 10:00. It was getting late for Mia and Elsa insisted that their chauffeur would drop her back to her stay.

The Journey of Soul

Just after Mia went, Elsa ran inside to open the gift that Mia had brought for her. As Elsa unwrapped, she found a few books within, and a beautiful journal to write. Mia gifted Elsa books on Buddhism, Stoicism and Bhagavad Gita (The Holy book of Hindus). Elsa's mobile rang and she received message from Mia, "Hope you liked the gift! Promise me that you will read them every weekend." Elsa promised to read them every weekend.

From that day onward, Elsa's life took an unexpected turn. She began to look beyond the superficial allure of pleasure and started to explore the richness of her own being. With each step on her path of self-discovery, she felt a sense of empowerment and freedom she had never known before.

The chance encounter with Mia had set Elsa on a transformative journey—one that would lead her to embrace the complexities of her own heart and to discover the true essence of happiness that lay beyond the pursuit of fleeting pleasures. As the pages of her books unfolded, Elsa would come to realize that the pursuit of self-discovery was not just a fleeting encounter but a lifelong adventure — a journey that would shape her perception of happiness, purpose, and fulfilment.

As Elsa continued to spend more time with Mia's books, she found herself embarking on an exhilarating journey of self-discovery. Guided by Mia's wisdom, she delved into the depths of her own being, unearthing layers of emotions, thoughts, and desires she had never fully explored before.

The process of self-discovery was not without its challenges. Elsa confronted her fears head-on, bravely facing the insecurities that had once held her back. She recognized that her pursuit of constant pleasure had been a way of avoiding these uncomfortable emotions, but now she was determined to embrace them, to understand them, and to grow from them.

In the safe space that Mia provided, Elsa acknowledged both her strengths and weaknesses. She realized that her vulnerabilities did not make her weak but rather were an integral part of her humanity. It was through acknowledging these vulnerabilities that she found the strength to overcome them, to face life's uncertainties with newfound resilience.

In her pursuit of self-discovery, Elsa explored new hobbies and passions. She rekindled her love for painting, finding solace and joy in the strokes of her brush as she expressed her inner thoughts and emotions on canvas. It was a form of therapy, a way for her to release the pent-up feelings that had remained hidden for so long.

She started taking pride in appearing for all her exams, that led to a vicious cycle of preparing and taking exams. Gradually, Elsa’s grades improved giving her a stable feeling of richness within her. It gave her a feeling that she is worthy and deserving and that she can do better next time. She started feeling courageous and came out of the veil of negativity.

Writing became yet another avenue for Elsa to explore her thoughts and emotions. She started keeping a journal, pouring her heart onto the pages without fear of judgment. Through journaling, she discovered the power of self-reflection, gaining insights into her own mind and learning to understand her own patterns of thought and behaviour. Elsa also compiled what she gathered from the books that

Mia gifted her, and wrote into her journal.

With Mia's gentle encouragement, Elsa learned to embrace creativity as a means of self-expression. She realized that true joy came from creating art for herself, without seeking validation or approval from others. It was liberating to break free from the constant need for external validation and to find fulfilment in the act of creation itself.

As Elsa ventured deeper into her journey of self-discovery, she began to shed the old layers of her identity, the persona she had built based on seeking pleasure and external validation. In doing so, she revealed a truer version of herself—a person of depth and authenticity, no longer defined by fleeting pleasures but by her willingness to explore her own complexities.

The path of self-discovery was not always smooth. There were moments of doubt and uncertainty, but Elsa knew she was on the right track. As she continued to grow and evolve, she discovered a sense of inner peace and contentment that she had never experienced before. She started processing and accepting her failures. Rather than perceiving failure as a negative outcome, she took it as valuable learning opportunity that allowed her to transcend setbacks and move forward with resilience. She also started embracing little imperfections of her body.

In the process of discovering herself, Elsa learned that happiness was not a destination to be reached but a journey to be embraced. It was about finding joy in the process of self-exploration, in understanding and accepting herself fully, and in pursuing passions that brought her genuine fulfilment.

The journey within became a profound and transformative experience for Elsa. It was a journey of self-acceptance, self-love, and self-empowerment. As she continued to explore her own depths, she realized that true happiness and fulfilment were not found in the pursuit of constant pleasure but in embracing the beauty and complexity of her own soul and proudly accepting highs and lows of one's life, owning them, treating them wherever required, and moving ahead with pride.

Our desires always disappoint us; for though we meet with something that gives us satisfaction, yet it never thoroughly answers our expectation." - Elbert Hubbard

Disconnecting In a Connected World

As Elsa navigated the intricate web of the digital world, she found herself grappling with the contrasting feelings of connection and disconnection. Social media platforms promise to bring people closer together, but as she scrolled through her feed, she realized that these virtual connections can never fully replace the warmth and authenticity of genuine human interactions.

Elsa reflected on her own experiences and those of her friends. The constant urge to stay online, to check notifications, and to be present on multiple social media platforms can be overwhelming. The fear of missing out (FOMO) pushed her to remain digitally connected even in the midst of physical gatherings. But she wondered, in the pursuit of staying connected online, are we unintentionally sacrificing the depth and richness of real-life connections?

As Elsa delved deeper, she observed the curated nature of social media. People often showcase only the highlights of their lives, creating an illusion of perfect happiness. She realized that this comparison-driven culture can lead to feelings of inadequacy and isolation. Elsa pondered if we were becoming more disconnected from our own authentic selves while striving to portray an idealized version of our lives to the world.

The more Elsa immersed herself in the virtual world, the more she became aware of the moments she's missing out on in real life. While attending events, she noticed people more engrossed in capturing the perfect photo for the social media likes and validation, than in experiencing the present moment. This made her wonder if the quest for validation through likes and comments is robbing us of the joy of fully participating in meaningful experiences. She wondered if all were destined to become digital robots one day. Something within her began to change as she started becoming appreciative of these things.

Despite the vast number of online friends and followers, Elsa experienced a sense of loneliness that lurked behind the screen. She remembered the times when she felt genuinely disconnected and isolated, even when surrounded by online connections. Her inner self began to question whether these virtual interactions can truly fill the void of real emotional connections.

Feeling a deep longing for genuine connections, Elsa starts making conscious efforts to disconnect from her devices and engage more with the world around her. She discovers the joy of face-to-face conversations, of sharing laughter and tears with friends in person, and of feeling truly heard and understood.

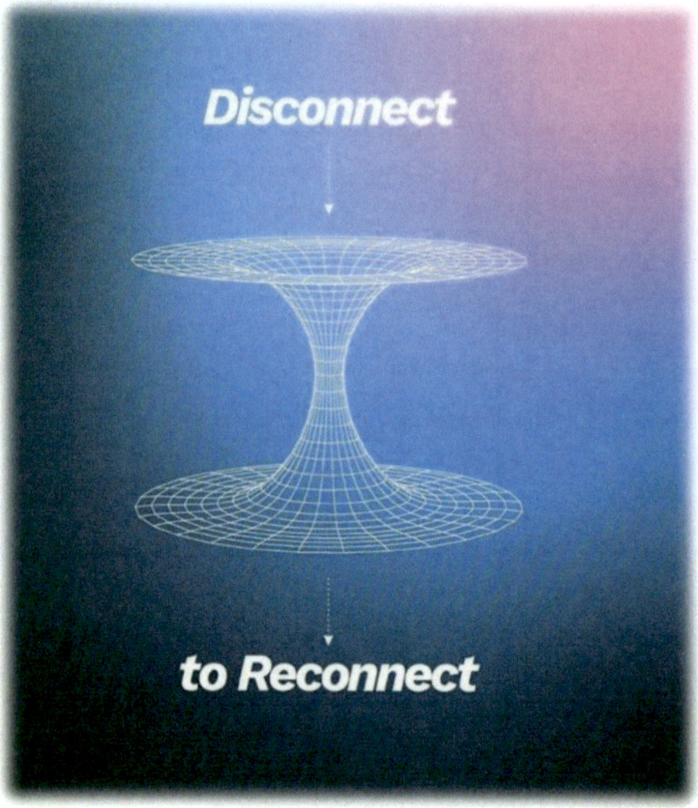

As she embarked on this journey of balancing her digital life with real-life experiences, Elsa carved out strategies to maintain a healthier relationship with technology. She encouraged setting boundaries for screen time, practicing digital detoxes, and being mindful of the impact of social media on emotional well-being. She started educating her peer groups about the negative impacts the prolonged screen time had on their health.

Elsa explored the value of nurturing deeper connections in the digital age. She indulged into the beauty of forming meaningful relationships, being an empathetic listener, and offering support to friends and loved ones in times of need. She discovered that genuine human interactions not only fulfil our emotional needs but also contribute to personal growth and a sense of belonging.

Embracing The Unpleasant

"You've failed again, darling!" declared Elsa's teacher Ms. Chelsea, as she felt bad about her performance in Mathematics. Earlier, though Elsa used to feel extreme remorse about such situations, but used to do nothing to improve her performance. Something had really changed within her. She replied, "Ms. Chelsea! I promise you shall see me clear my exams with good scores next time". Ms. Chelsea was Mrs. Reed's friend and like a second mother to Elsa. She was taken aback with Elsa's reply and was happy that at least Elsa was ready to take the responsibility.

After the school ended Elsa came to Ms. Chelsea and requested her to give her remedial classes for about an hour every day except weekends at the comfortability of latter's home, to which Ms. Chelsea readily agreed and said, "I would come at your place only, don't you worry about that". Ms. Chelsea also wanted to discuss the positive change in Elsa's behaviour with Mrs. Reed. "Your mother would be happy to see me" she added. Elsa smiled and nodded as a gesture to welcome her.

It was about 4 pm during the day and the door bell rang. It was Ms. Chelsea as expected. Elsa's teacher started coming every day and helped her in problem areas for her subject. Ms. Chelsea also discussed many other aspects of Elsa's life that she had to offer. She advised her to start helping her house helps and be polite with them. She also advised her to spend more time with her family and friends by meeting them physically rather then being connected on phone. "Our phones should only be for emergencies and for those times when we wish to connect to someone who is far away from us!" said Mrs. Chelsea. This reminded Elsa of Mia and she texted her immediately that this time she would try to do good in mathematics.

As Elsa delved further into her journey of self-discovery, she came to a profound realization: life was not solely about seeking pleasure, but about embracing the entirety of the human experience the good, the bad, and the ugly. In the past, she had often shied away from anything that brought discomfort or pain, seeking only moments of joy and happiness. But now, she understood that true growth and self-awareness came from confronting the challenges that life presented, no matter how unpleasant they might be.

As Elsa continued to grow and evolve, she found herself facing one of the most significant challenges of adolescence: peer pressure. She delved into her personal experiences of grappling with societal norms and the overwhelming desire to fit in with her peers. She tried to resist the pressures around her, and embracing her authentic self, even when it meant going against the crowd.

Elsa experienced conflicting emotions when confronted with peer pressure. The pressure to conform to societal expectations, trends, and behaviours that were incredibly intense during her teenage years. However, she also recognized the importance of staying true to her own values and beliefs.

Elsa's journey began with the fear of 'Being Different' and went through finding Courage in individuality. She once found herself changing aspects of her personality or interests to fit in with certain groups. There were instances when she felt afraid of standing out, fearing rejection or ridicule from her peers. This fear of being different, she realized, is a common thread among teenagers striving to find their place in the world. Eventually, she stood up for her friends who were facing peer pressure. She discussed with them the importance of supporting one another and fostering an environment where everyone feels comfortable being authentic.

Elsa also emphasized the importance of self-expression as a means to combat peer pressure. Whether it's through her hobbies, interests, or personal style, she discovers that embracing her identity sets her apart in the best way possible, attracting friends who appreciate her for who she genuinely is. She recounted various social situations where peer pressure is prevalent, such as parties, group outings, and school events. She explored the various ways teenagers may feel pressured to engage in risky behaviours, and how she learned to trust her instincts and make responsible choices.

With newfound courage, Elsa faced her fears and insecurities head-on. She no longer ran from difficult emotions but rather embraced them as opportunities for growth. It was not an easy journey; there were moments of vulnerability and discomfort, but each step she took in facing her inner struggles strengthened her resolve.

Through this process, Elsa learned that vulnerability was not a weakness, but a source of strength. By acknowledging her own imperfections and being open about her struggles, she found that she connected with others on a deeper level. It was in these moments of vulnerability that true bonds were formed, and she discovered the power of authentic connections. Some connections were deep that were actually with her own soul. *Some such connections led to the realisation that there lies a perseverant soul in every body, realisation only wakes her up!*

As Elsa continued to explore her own depths, she also sought to understand the experiences of those around her. She reconnected with old friends and family, taking the time to listen to their stories, joys, and pains. As she offered her support and empathy, she realized the profound impact these connections had on her sense of fulfilment. Helping others led to an elevated sense of self- worth.

She learned that meaningful relationships were not just about sharing moments of pleasure but about being present for one another during life's highs and lows. In lending a helping hand or a compassionate ear, she found a sense of purpose and fulfilment that mere pleasures could never match. Elsa journey of embracing the unpleasant also extended beyond her personal relationships. She began to challenge herself in various aspects of life, seeking out opportunities for growth and self-improvement. She faced academic challenges with determination, tackling subjects she once found daunting and pushing herself to excel.

Outside her comfort zone, Elsa engaged in community service, dedicating her time and effort to causes she cared deeply about. As she volunteered in local shelters and community programs, she witnessed the resilience of others facing adversity and discovered the strength that came from collective support.

With each new experience, Elsa grew more resilient, more compassionate, and more authentic. The pursuit of pleasure, once her sole focus, had now evolved into a broader quest for meaning and purpose. Embracing the full spectrum of human emotions and experiences enriched her life in ways she could never have imagined.

As she continued to navigate her journey of self-discovery, Elsa understood that life was a tapestry woven from both moments of pleasure and moments of discomfort. By embracing the unpleasant, she found the courage to step into her own power, unapologetically embracing the complexity of her emotions and experiences.

In the tapestry of life, she realized that each thread, whether joyful or painful, was an essential part of her story. Through the pursuit of self-awareness, meaningful connections, and embracing the challenges life presented, she discovered a sense of fulfilment that surpassed the fleeting pleasures she once sought. Elsa had unlocked a profound truth—that in embracing the entirety of her human experience, she had found a path to genuine happiness and what she called a life of Zero Pleasure.

Transformation Within

"Elsa! We have formed a new group for those who are interested in the upcoming concert of the new band", shouted Olivia, from the other corner of the classroom, "come, join us, why are you sitting at that corner?" It was a matter of immense excitement for all the students of her class. But Elsa had a flat reaction. "You carry on", said she, to her friends. "I will stay back at home. I had ordered some new flower pots, need to finish some gardening in the backyard today."

"Oh, come on Elsa! What has happened to you? It's "The Band, the one that all of us have been waiting for since years, to come to Beverly Hills. And now, when the day arrives, you wanna stay back!?" said Olivia. Olivia is Elsa's best friend forever. They have known each other for last 13 years. Their mothers are friends too. Olivia has a fancy family background. Her father was once a soccer player with Elsa's father but could not be selected in the Nationals team. However, it never affected their healthy friendship and Mr. Marcus was still ready to do anything for Olivia's father.

"Please understand Olivia, in fact, I would urge you too to stay with me", said Elsa. But what has changed in Elsa so much that she has started approaching more within herself and less to the outside distractions, thought Olivia. How can she be so inspired, and what is inspiring her so much? Olivia had many such questions echoing in her mind since many months that she wanted to discuss with Elsa but Elsa always took her discussion to Mia that made Olivia jealous and then she used to switch over the topic.

Elsa's journey of self-discovery had been a profound and transformative experience, one that had unravelled the layers of her being and revealed a truer version of herself. As she continued to navigate this path of growth, each day brought her closer to a newfound sense of connectedness with herself and the world around her.

It was not a journey without challenges or setbacks. There were moments of doubt and uncertainty, but she had learned to embrace them as opportunities for growth and learning. With the guidance of Mia and the wisdom she had gained through self-exploration, Elsa found the strength to persist.

As she transformed from a pleasure-seeking girl to a young woman on a quest for meaning, Elsa's inner radiance began to shine brighter than ever before. Her friends noticed the change in her, the newfound sense of purpose and authenticity that emanated from within. They were drawn to her, curious about the transformation she had undergone.

Inspired by Elsa's journey, Olivia and her friends began to question their own pursuits of superficial pleasures. She became a catalyst for them to seek more profound experiences beyond the fleeting highs of instant gratification. Together, Olivia and Elsa engaged in heartfelt conversations about the meaning of life, the importance of self-awareness, and the power of human connection.

In the midst of their shared explorations, Elsa realized the significance of her own transformation. It was not just about her individual growth; it was about the ripple effect she had on the lives of those around her. Through her own journey, she had inadvertently become a source of inspiration for others.

Her newfound perspective on life led Elsa to cherish the little things that had once gone unnoticed in her pursuit of pleasure. She found joy in the simplicity of a heartfelt conversation with a friend, the warmth of a hug that conveyed more than words ever could, and the beauty of nature that revealed the wonders of existence.

Elsa began to immerse herself in the present moment, savouring each experience with a newfound appreciation. She no longer rushed through life in search of the next thrill, but instead, she allowed herself to fully embrace every facet of the journey.

In moments of stillness, she would sit under the canopy of stars, marvelling at the vastness of the universe and her place within it. She discovered a sense of interconnectedness with the world, realizing that her journey of self-discovery was intertwined with the collective tapestry of human existence.

Life was no longer just about seeking pleasure; it had become a profound exploration of purpose and meaning. Elsa embraced all that life had to offer— the highs and the lows, the joys and the sorrows, the challenges and the triumphs. She learned to view every experience as an opportunity for growth and learning, finding beauty in the process of becoming.

With each passing day, she felt a growing sense of fulfilment that surpassed the temporary gratifications she had once sought. The pursuit of pleasure had been replaced with a higher calling—the pursuit of self-awareness and a life lived with purpose.

As she continued to inspire those around her with her newfound perspective, Elsa realized the power of her own journey. She had undergone a major transformation that extended far beyond her individual self. Her quest for self-discovery had become a beacon of light for others, guiding them towards a more authentic and meaningful existence.

In the end, Elsa had found that true happiness came not from seeking constant pleasure, but from embracing the beauty of life's intricacies. She had discovered that life was a tapestry of experiences, woven with threads of joy, sorrow, and everything in between. And in the midst of it all, she had found her own unique place—a place of purpose, connection, and a newfound perspective that had forever changed the course of her life.

Zero Pleasures, Infinite Fulfilment

Madam Chelsea and friends of Elsa were stunned at the progress that she made in the subjects that she struggled with earlier. “Good job, keep it up!” said Ms. Chelsea.

The school had organised a workshop on Environment where Elsa was the activist leader and volunteer. She urged everyone to plant at least one tree a month and take care of nurturing it. In the end, Elsa was to deliver her speech on environmental issues.

“… Single use plastic is the major culprit that adds on to the environmental pollution. Decrease the use of single use plastic to the bare minimum if you wish to see your future generations happy. Boycott plastic! If you love your planet.” Elsa’s speech ended followed by a huge applaud by the audience.

As Elsa’s journey of self-discovery drew to a close, she had come to a profound understanding of what "zero pleasures" truly meant. It wasn't about denying oneself happiness or enjoyment; rather, it was a liberation from the constant chase of shallow and temporary pleasures that had once dictated her life. She had learned to find contentment in the present moment, to appreciate the beauty of simplicity, and to cultivate true fulfilment from within.

In the past, Elsa had believed that the key to happiness lay in accumulating external pleasures—a never-ending quest for more, driven by the pursuit of instant gratification. However, her transformative journey had unveiled the fallacy of this belief. The superficial highs she had once sought were ephemeral, leaving her yearning for more without ever experiencing lasting fulfilment.

Elsa had set herself free from the chains of constant craving. She found that true happiness and fulfilment were not found in the pursuit of external validations or possessions, but rather in the depth of her own being. By focusing on self-discovery and inner growth, she had cultivated a sense of contentment that no fleeting pleasure could match.

Her experiences had shown her that happiness was not a destination to be reached, but a state of being cultivated through mindfulness and gratitude for the present moment. She learned to find joy in the little things—the warmth of a sunrise, the laughter of loved ones, and the serenity of a quiet moment alone with her thoughts. These simple yet profound experiences brought a sense of fulfilment that transcended the transient allure of external pleasures.

Throughout her journey, Elsa had come to understand that true happiness and fulfilment were not reliant on external circumstances, but rather on her own perspective and attitude towards life. She had taken the time to confront her fears, embrace her vulnerabilities, and explore her passions, thus uncovering the true essence of her authentic self.

In this newfound state of being, Elsa became a beacon of inspiration for those around her. Her friends witnessed her transformation and found themselves inspired to seek a deeper and more meaningful existence. She encouraged them to question their own pursuits, to discover their passions, and to embark on their own journeys of self-discovery.

Elsa's life became a living testament to the power of authenticity and self- awareness. She had freed herself from the chains of external expectations, no longer seeking approval or validation from others. Instead, she was guided by her inner compass, living life on her terms and finding fulfilment in the pursuit of her true passions.

As she reflected on her journey, she understood that the pursuit of pleasure alone was an endless loop of desires, never leading to lasting contentment. In embracing the philosophy of "zero pleasures," she had found a path to infinite fulfilment—a life lived with purpose, intention, and a profound appreciation for the richness of every moment.

Her story served as a reminder that true happiness and fulfilment were not elusive concepts but attainable states of being that resided within each individual. Elsa's journey had shown her that by cultivating self-awareness, embracing vulnerability, and savouring life's simple joys, one could discover the infinite well of fulfilment that lay within oneself.

With her heart full of gratitude and her spirit soaring with newfound purpose, Elsa Reed had embarked on a life defined by zero pleasures and infinite fulfilment—a life where the pursuit of self-discovery and authenticity were the guiding lights, illuminating the path to genuine happiness and a sense of purpose that transcended the boundaries of time and space. She was joyous and cheerful, and lead her life happily without seeking validation from anyone.

Excerpts from Elsa's Journal

Buddhism and Zero Pleasures

In Buddhism, the concept of "zero pleasures" is closely related to the teachings on suffering and the impermanent nature of all things. Buddhism acknowledges the existence of pleasures and desires in the world, but it also emphasizes that these pleasures are temporary and ultimately lead to suffering. The pursuit of sensory pleasures, according to Buddhism, can perpetuate the cycle of craving, attachment, and dissatisfaction.

The Four Noble Truths, one of the fundamental teachings in Buddhism, lay the groundwork for understanding the concept of zero pleasures:

1. ***The Truth of Suffering (Dukkha)***: Buddhism recognizes that life is marked by various forms of suffering, dissatisfaction, and unsatisfaction. Even the most pleasurable experiences are impermanent and subject to change, leading to a sense of dissatisfaction.

2. ***The Truth of the Origin of Suffering (Samudaya)***: The second noble truth points to desire, attachment, and craving as the root causes of suffering. Desires and attachments to sensory pleasures are seen as contributing to the perpetuation of suffering.

3. ***The Truth of the Cessation of Suffering (Nirodha)***: The third noble truth offers hope by suggesting that there is a way to end suffering. This can be achieved by letting go of desires and attachments that lead to suffering.

While pursuing pleasure can bring joy and fulfilment, it is essential to strike a balance and avoid excesses that may lead to negative consequences. Enjoy the simple and meaningful pleasures that life has to offer, and let them enrich your journey towards happiness and contentment.

4. ***The Truth of the Path to the Cessation of Suffering (Magga)*:** The fourth noble truth outlines the Eightfold Path, which serves as a guide for living a life that is free from craving and attachment, leading to the cessation of suffering.

In Buddhism, the pursuit of genuine happiness and contentment lies not in external sensory pleasures but in cultivating inner qualities and mental states that lead to true peace and liberation. This is achieved through practices such as meditation, mindfulness, compassion, and wisdom.

The concept of "zero pleasures" in Buddhism does not advocate for a life of asceticism or complete denial of all pleasures. Instead, it encourages individuals to be mindful of their desires and attachments, recognizing their impermanent and unsatisfactory nature. By understanding the transient nature of pleasures, one can develop a deeper sense of contentment and peace that is not dependent on external circumstances.

The ultimate goal in Buddhism is to attain Nirvana, which is the state of liberation from the cycle of birth and death *(samsara)* and the end of all suffering. Nirvana is often described as a state of perfect peace and freedom, beyond the realm of ordinary pleasures and pains.

In conclusion, Buddhism's perspective on "zero pleasures" underscores the impermanence of sensory gratification and the potential for suffering associated with attachment to such pleasures. By cultivating inner qualities and understanding the true nature of desires, individuals can embark on a path toward genuine happiness and liberation from suffering.

Zero Pleasures and Stoicism

In Stoicism, the concept of "zero pleasures" aligns closely with the philosophy's emphasis on virtue, self-control, and the pursuit of inner tranquillity. Stoicism, founded in ancient Greece and later developed in ancient Rome, teaches that true happiness and fulfilment come from living in harmony with nature and accepting the things that are beyond our control. Pleasures and desires are seen as external and fleeting, and the Stoics believed that attaching ourselves to them can lead to unnecessary suffering and disturbances of the soul.

The Stoic approach to pleasures can be summarized in the following key principles:

1. ***Tranquillity and Apatheia***: Stoicism advocates for achieving tranquillity of the mind (ataraxia) and inner peace. To attain this state, the Stoics practiced apatheia, which does not mean complete lack of emotions, but rather a sense of emotional detachment from external events and outcomes. By not being overly affected by pleasures or pains, one can achieve a more steady and balanced emotional state.

2. ***Virtue as the Highest Good***: The Stoics believed that the highest good, or the ultimate goal in life, is to live a virtuous life. Virtue, as defined by Stoicism, includes qualities such as wisdom, courage, justice, and temperance. Pleasures, especially those associated with material possessions or sensual gratification, were considered inferior and often distractions from the pursuit of virtue.

3. ***Hedonic Adaptation***: Stoicism recognized the phenomenon of hedonic adaptation, which refers to the tendency of humans to quickly return to a baseline level of happiness after experiencing either pleasure or pain. This understanding led the Stoics to question the value of pursuing external pleasures that are short-lived and do not lead to lasting contentment.

4. ***Control Over Desires***: According to Stoicism, individuals should focus their efforts on what they can control, which is their own attitudes and choices. By mastering their desires and aligning them with reason and virtue, individuals can find greater contentment and freedom from the constant pursuit of pleasures.

5. ***Inner Freedom*:** Stoicism promotes the idea of inner freedom or autonomy (autarkeia). This inner freedom comes from recognizing that the only things within our control are our judgments and responses to external events, not the events themselves. By freeing ourselves from the attachment to pleasures and external circumstances, we can find greater peace and self-mastery.

It is important to note that Stoicism does not advocate for complete abstinence from all pleasures. Instead, it encourages individuals to be moderate in their pursuit of pleasure and to avoid becoming enslaved by desires or dependent on external goods for their well-being.

By focusing on inner virtue and inner tranquillity, Stoicism offers a path to a more resilient and fulfilling life, regardless of external circumstances or the presence of pleasures. Embracing the concept of "zero pleasures" in Stoicism means recognizing the impermanence and superficiality of external gratifications and finding true contentment through the cultivation of wisdom, virtue, and a well-disciplined mind.

Concept of Zero Pleasures and Bhagavad Gita

The Bhagavad Gita primarily focuses on imparting spiritual wisdom and guidance to Prince Arjuna, who is facing a moral dilemma on the battlefield of Kurukshetra. The teachings revolve around the following key themes:

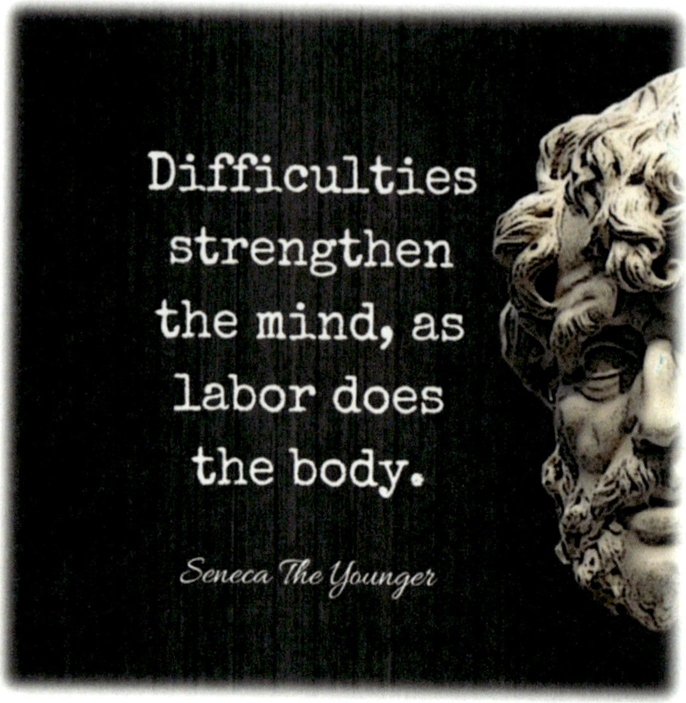

1. ***Detachment and Renunciation***: The Bhagavad Gita emphasizes the importance of practicing detachment *(vairagya)* from the outcomes of actions. By doing so, one can maintain equanimity in the face of pleasure and pain, success and failure. This detachment is not a rejection of pleasures but rather a non-attachment to the results of actions, enabling one to perform their duties with a sense of equanimity. A popular Hindu saying goes, *"Karm karo, fal ki chinta mat karo*", is derived from Bhagavad Gita, that is written in its Chapter 2, Verse 47, कर्मण्येवाधिकारस्ते मा फलेषु कदाचन मा कर्मफलहेतुर्भूर्मा ते सङ्गोऽस्त्वकर्मणि।

2. ***Pursuit of Self-Realization***: The central message of the Bhagavad Gita is the pursuit of self-realization and

understanding the true nature of the self *(Atman)* as eternal and beyond the physical body. Through self-knowledge and spiritual practice, one can transcend material desires and seek lasting inner contentment and joy.

3. ***Karma Yoga*:** The Gita introduces the concept of Karma Yoga, the yoga of selfless action. By performing one's duties and responsibilities without attachment to the outcomes, an individual can free themselves from the bondage of desires and attain a state of inner peace.

4. ***Sannyasa and Tyaga*:** The Bhagavad Gita speaks about the paths of renunciation (sannyasa) and relinquishment *(tyaga)*. While these paths involve giving up attachments, they are not about suppressing desires but about redirecting them towards higher spiritual goals.

5. ***Devotion (Bhakti)*:** The Gita also extols the path of devotion to the divine. By surrendering oneself to a higher power and practicing sincere devotion, one can find solace and liberation from worldly attachments.

Though the Bhagavad Gita does not specifically discuss "zero pleasures" as a concept, its teachings encourage individuals to transcend the pursuit of fleeting sensory pleasures and to seek higher truths and spiritual fulfilment. The focus is on cultivating inner virtues, selflessness, and a deeper connection with the divine, which leads to a state of lasting contentment and spiritual liberation.

Zero Pleasures

In a world where dreams take flight,
As a teenage girl, I seek delight,
So many pleasures, my heart does yearn,
To discover, explore, and to learn.

First, the joys of friendship, warm and true,
Laughing together, sharing secrets too,
Through ups and downs, we stand by each other's side,
In a bond of sisterhood, we find our pride.

Next, the thrill of adventure, wild and free,
Exploring new places, where no one else may be,
With curiosity as my compass and courage in my soul,
I chase the unknown, making every moment whole.

Then comes love, the sweetest of all emotions,
Fluttering butterflies, like a dance in slow motion,
A tender touch, a stolen gaze, hearts aflutter,
In this enchanting realm, my heart finds its utopia.

Ah, music, the rhythm of my soul's refrain,
In lyrics and melodies, my emotions gain,
Lost in its melodies, I find my escape,
Through joyful highs and melancholy's landscape.

Zero Pleasures

The wonders of art, colours on a canvas spread,
Expressing feelings unsaid, where words may dread,
With brush strokes and sketches, my emotions speak,
On the canvas of life, I paint dreams unique.

Books, portals to worlds unknown,
Where imagination blooms and stories are sown,
In each chapter, a new universe unfurls,
Transporting me to magical worlds.

And then, there's self-discovery, a journey profound,
Unravelling passions, as life's mysteries abound,
Embracing strengths, quirks, and flaws with glee,
As I blossom into the woman I'm meant to be.

Yet, amidst these pleasures, let's not forget,
The simple joys, the little things we get,
A warm cup of tea, a starry night's gaze,
A hug from a loved one on gloomy days.

So many pleasures in this life I seek,
As a teenage girl, with each day, I peek,
Into the future, where dreams take flight,
Embracing life's treasures, with all my might.

About the Author

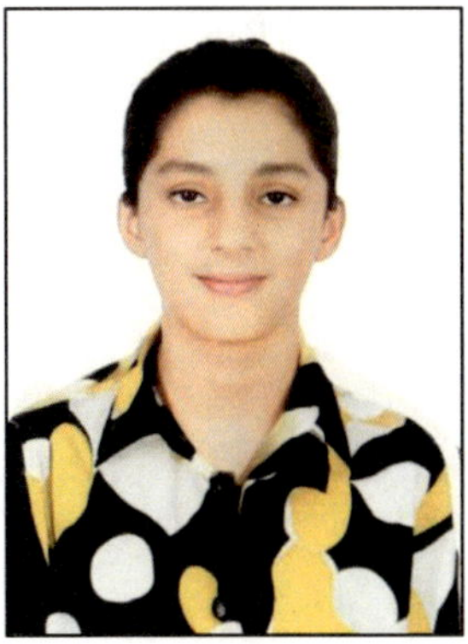

Ayana Thakran, at the age of just 13, is a name that resonates with creativity, intellect, and an insatiable thirst for knowledge. Currently a bright student in the 8th grade, author's journey is nothing short of inspiring as she effortlessly navigates both the realms of academia and artistic expression.

With a natural inclination towards daring the challenges, Ayana has carved her path by participating in prestigious events such as school Olympiads (SOF) and has achieved various medals by the age of 9 years. Her keen analytical skills and scientific curiosity have not only earned her accolades but also showcased her potential to become a formidable force in the world.

Author's voracious appetite for learning extends to diverse arenas. She has a natural instinct of an orater. She loves to read books and novels. Ayana is not bound by the geographical boundaries of the world and is readily open to accept the cosmopolitan trends and languages. Her recent hobbies are writing and learning to read and write Korean language by herself. Music is her soul. She loves to listen to her favorite collection of songs.

Ayana is a curious teenager who gets the inspiration of standing firm from her mother. She strongly believes in the poem by Shri Sohanlal Dwivedi, "lehron se dar kar kashti paar nahin hoti, koshish karne walon ki kabhi haar nahin hoti", which means, 'Keep trying until you suceed, never give up!'

Lots of Love!!